SCOTTISH CERTIFICATE OF EDUCATION

Credit
MATHEMATICS

The Scottish Certificate of Education Examination Papers
are reprinted by special permission of
THE SCOTTISH QUALIFICATIONS AUTHORITY

Note: The answers to the questions do not emanate from the Authority.

ISBN 0 7169 9273 6
© *Robert Gibson & Sons, Glasgow, Ltd., 1998*

ROBERT GIBSON · Publisher
17 Fitzroy Place, Glasgow, G3 7SF.

SCOTTISH CERTIFICATE OF EDUCATION

MATHEMATICS

Standard Grade — CREDIT LEVEL

Time: 2 hours 15 minutes

INSTRUCTIONS TO CANDIDATES

1. Answer as many questions as you can.

2. Full credit will be given only where the solution contains appropriate working.

3. Square-ruled paper is provided.

FORMULAE LIST

The roots of $ax^2 + bx + c = 0$ are $x = \dfrac{-b \pm \sqrt{b^2 - 4ac}}{2a}$

Sine rule: $\dfrac{a}{\sin A} = \dfrac{b}{\sin B} = \dfrac{c}{\sin C}$

Cosine rule: $a^2 = b^2 + c^2 - 2bc \cos A$ or $\cos A = \dfrac{b^2 + c^2 - a^2}{2bc}$

Area of a triangle: Area $= \dfrac{1}{2} ab \sin C$

Trigonometric relationships: $\dfrac{\sin x°}{\cos x°} = \tan x° ; \sin^2 x° + \cos^2 x° = 1$

SCOTTISH
CERTIFICATE OF
EDUCATION
1993

TUESDAY, 11 MAY
1.30 PM – 3.45 PM

MATHEMATICS
STANDARD GRADE
Credit Level

	KU	RA

1. The diagram shows a tent.

The shape of the material used to make the tent is a sector of a circle as shown below.

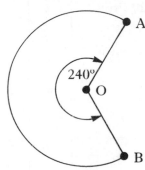

O is the centre of the circle.

OA and OB are radii of length 3 metres.

Angle AOB is 240°.

Calculate the area of this piece of material.

3

2. One hundred milligrams of a drug are given to a patient.

At the end of each hour the number of milligrams of the drug left in the body is 10% less than at the beginning of that hour.

How many milligrams of the drug are left in the body at the end of four hours?

3

3. The total number of visitors to an exhibition was $2 \cdot 925 \times 10^7$.

The exhibition was open each day from 5 June to 29 September **inclusive**.

Calculate the average number of visitors per day to the exhibition.

3

4. An extract from a camping holiday brochure is shown below.

| Season | For 14 nights | | | | | Over 14 nights |
	Two adults	Each extra adult	Each young adult aged 14 to 17	Each child aged 10 to 13	Each child aged 0 to 9	Each additional night per family
Low	£399	£74	£40	Free	Free	£19
Mid	£555	£85	£50	Free	Free	£29
High	£699	£95	£60	£46	Free	£39

(a) Find the cost of a holiday for 2 adults and a child, aged 8, for 17 nights during mid season.

(b) Write down a formula to find the cost, £C, of a holiday in mid season for 2 adults and a child aged 8 lasting t nights, where t is greater than 14.

5. A tank contains 240 litres of water.

When the tap is opened, water flows from the tank at a steady rate of 20 litres per minute.

(a) On the 2 mm square-ruled paper provided, draw a graph of the volume, V litres, of water in the tank against the time, t minutes.

(b) Write down an equation connecting V and t.

6. The following number pattern can be used to sum consecutive square whole numbers.

$$1^2 + 2^2 = \frac{2 \times 3 \times 5}{6}$$

$$1^2 + 2^2 + 3^2 = \frac{3 \times 4 \times 7}{6}$$

$$1^2 + 2^2 + 3^2 + 4^2 = \frac{4 \times 5 \times 9}{6}$$

(a) Express $1^2 + 2^2 + 3^2 + \ldots + 10^2$ in the same way.

(b) Express $1^2 + 2^2 + 3^2 + \ldots + n^2$ in the same way.

KU	RA
	2
	3
3	
2	
	1
	2

	KU	RA

7. Solve the system of equations

$$5a + 3b = 9$$

$$7a - 2b = 25.$$

3

8.

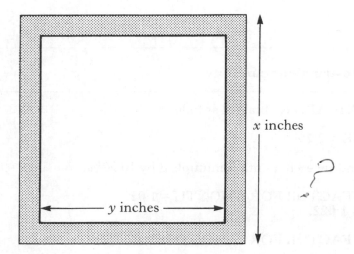

x inches

y inches

A square picture frame is shown above.

The border of the frame (shaded in the diagram) has uniform width and an area of 48 square inches.

(a) Show that $(x - y)(x + y) = 48$.

2

(b) Given that x and y are whole numbers each greater than 10, find suitable replacements for x and y.

3

9. The diagram opposite shows two storage jars which are mathematically similar.

The volume of the large jar is 1·2 litres.

Find the volume of the smaller jar.

Give your answer in litres correct to 2 significant figures.

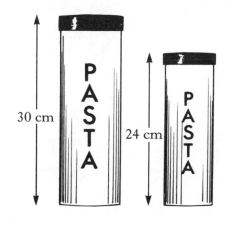

30 cm

24 cm

4

10. The table below shows some interest rates for credit cards.

		KU	RA

CREDIT CARD INTEREST RATES

Name of Card	Monthly Rate	Annual Percentage Rate (APR)
FLEXICARD	2·2%	29·8%
SHOPCARD	2·1%	
TRUSTYCARD		23·9%

Read the following instructions carefully

The APR for FLEXICARD is obtained as follows:

MONTHLY RATE = 2·2%.

The amount outstanding each month is multiplied by 102·2%.

MULTIPLYING FACTOR FOR 1 MONTH = 1·022
because 102·2% = 1·022.

MULTIPLYING FACTOR FOR 12 MONTHS = $(1·022)^{12}$.

$(1·022)^{12}$ = 1·298 CORRECT TO 3 DECIMAL PLACES.

The APR is therefore 29·8% correct to one decimal place.

(a)   Use the instructions shown above to calculate the APR for SHOPCARD.   2

(b)   Calculate the **monthly rate** for TRUSTYCARD.   4

11. A traffic island, ABC, is shown below.

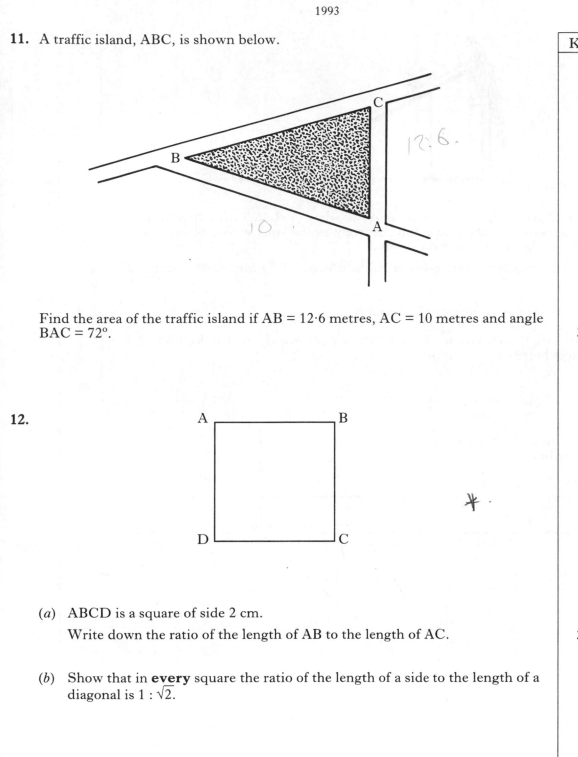

Find the area of the traffic island if AB = 12·6 metres, AC = 10 metres and angle BAC = 72°.

KU	RA
2	

12.

(a) ABCD is a square of side 2 cm.

Write down the ratio of the length of AB to the length of AC.

(b) Show that in **every** square the ratio of the length of a side to the length of a diagonal is 1 : √2.

KU	RA
2	
	3

13.

The time, T seconds, taken by a child to slide down a chute varies directly as the length, L metres, of the chute and inversely as the square root of the height, H metres, of the chute above the ground.

It takes 10 seconds to slide down a chute which is 3·75 metres long and 2·25 metres high.

(a) Find a formula connecting T, L and H.

3

(b) How long does it take to slide down a chute which is 5 metres long and 2·56 metres high?

2

14. The diagram shows the goalposts on a rugby field.

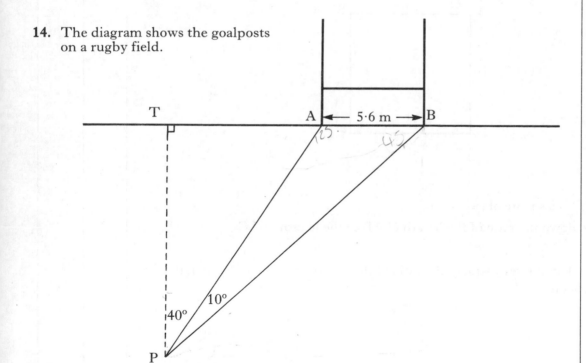

To take a kick at goal, a player moves from T to position P.

TP is perpendicular to TB.
Angle TPA = 40° and angle APB = 10°.

The distance AB between the goal posts is 5·6 metres.

Find the distance from T to P.

6

		KU	RA

15. (a) Multiply out the brackets and simplify

$$(3a + 2b)(5a - 4b).$$

KU **2**

(b) Solve the equation

$$2x^2 + 5x - 12 = 0.$$

KU **3**

16. The volume of water, V millions of gallons, stored in a reservoir during any month is to be predicted by using the formula

$$V = 1 + 0.5 \cos (30t)°$$

where t is the number of the month. (For January $t = 1$, February $t = 2 \ldots$)

(a) Find the volume of water in the reservoir in October.

RA **3**

(b) The local council would need to consider water rationing during any month in which the volume of water stored is likely to be less than 0.55 million gallons.

Will the local council need to consider water rationing?

Justify your answer.

RA **3**

17. (a) A function f is given by
$$f(x) = 4^x.$$

Find the value of $f\left(\frac{3}{2}\right)$.

KU **2**

(b) Express $\sqrt{32} + \sqrt{8}$ as a surd in its simplest form.

KU **3**

18. The total time a walk takes in hillwalking depends on the horizontal distance covered (*h* kilometres) and the vertical height climbed (*v* metres).

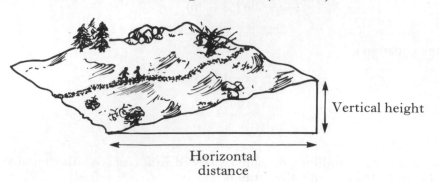

Vertical height

Horizontal
distance

For **each kilometre** of horizontal distance, 12 minutes should be allowed.

(*a*) (i) Write down the time which should be allowed for *h* kilometres of horizontal distance.

| | | **1** | |

(ii) For **each 100 metres** of vertical height, 10 minutes should be allowed.

Write down the time which should be allowed for *v* metres of vertical height.

| | | | **2** |

(iii) Show that the **total** time *T* **hours** which should be allowed for the walk is given by the formula

$$T = \frac{120\,h + v}{600}.$$

| | | | **3** |

(*b*) For safety reasons, hillwalkers should be off the hills by 1900 hours.

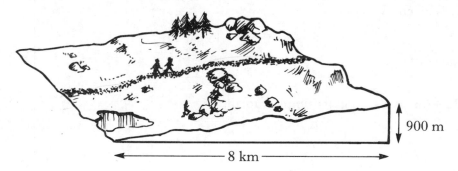

900 m

8 km

Would it be safe to start the walk shown above at 1300 hours?

Justify your answer.

| | | | **3** |

[END OF QUESTION PAPER]

SCOTTISH
CERTIFICATE OF
EDUCATION
1994

WEDNESDAY, 11 MAY
1.30 PM – 3.45 PM

MATHEMATICS
STANDARD GRADE
Credit Level

	KU	RA

1. Solve the equation

$$5 + 3a = a - 15.$$

KU: 3

2. The number of people suffering from a virus is 12 million.

For each of the next three years, the number of people suffering from the virus is expected to be 5% more than the number in the previous year.

How many people are expected to be suffering from the virus in 3 years time?

Give your answer in millions.

KU: 3

3. The Scott family want to build a conservatory as shown below.

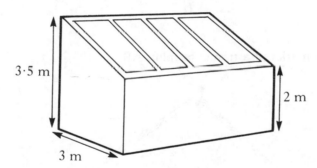

3·5 m

2 m

3 m

The conservatory is to be 3 metres wide. The height of the conservatory at the lower end is to be 2 metres and at the higher end 3·5 metres.

To obtain planning permission, the roof must slope at an angle of (25 ± 2) degrees to the horizontal.

Should planning permission be granted?

Justify your answer.

RA: 4

4. The diagram opposite shows
two parallel lines meeting a
third at 72°.

(*a*) Find the value of *b*.

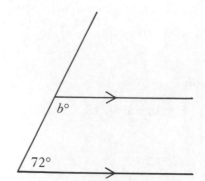

(*b*) The diagram opposite shows
the general case of two parallel
lines meeting a third line.

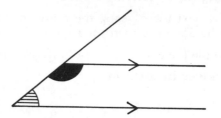

Prove that, in every case, the sum of the shaded angles is 180°.

5. A loop of rope is used to mark out a triangular plot, ABC.

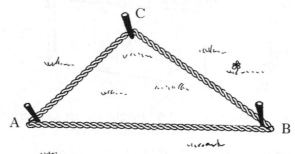

The loop of rope measures 6 metres.

Pegs are positioned at A and B such that AB is 2·5 metres.

The third peg is positioned at C such that BC is 2 metres.

Prove that angle ACB = 90°.

Do not use a scale drawing.

KU	RA
1	
	3
4	

6. The sequence of odd numbers starting with 3 is 3, 5, 7, 9, 11, . . .

Consecutive numbers from this sequence can be added using the following pattern

$$3 + 5 + 7 + 9 = \mathbf{4 \times 6}$$
$$3 + 5 + 7 + 9 + 11 = \mathbf{5 \times 7}$$
$$3 + 5 + 7 + 9 + 11 + 13 = \mathbf{6 \times 8}$$

(a) Express $3 + 5 + \ldots + 25$ in the same way.

(b) The first n numbers in this sequence are added. Find a formula for the total.

KU	RA
	2
	3

7. A planet takes 88 days to travel round the Sun.

The approximate path of the planet round the Sun is a circle with diameter 1.2×10^7 kilometres.

Find the speed of the planet as it travels round the Sun.

Give your answer in kilometres per hour, correct to 2 significant figures.

KU	RA
4	

8. The diagram below shows the cross-section of a petrol tank.

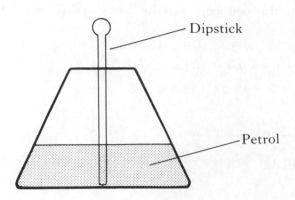

Dipstick

Petrol

A dipstick is used to check the level of the petrol in the tank.

The dipstick has marks to show empty (E), quarter full ($\frac{1}{4}$), half full ($\frac{1}{2}$), three quarters full ($\frac{3}{4}$) and totally full (F).

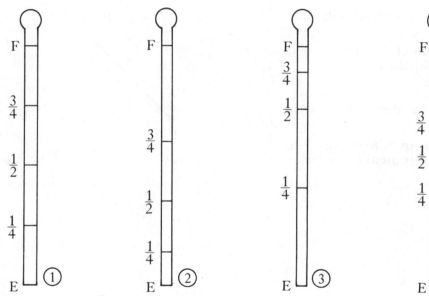

(a) Which dipstick, ①—④, should be used with the tank?

Explain your answer fully.

(b) Here is another petrol tank.

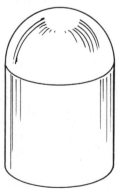

Sketch a graph to show how the depth of the petrol varies with the volume of petrol in the tank.

	KU	RA

9. (a) Remove the brackets and simplify

$$(2y - 3)^2.$$

KU **2**

(b) Factorise $2x^2 + 7x - 4$.

KU **2**

10. A sensor in a security system covers a horizontal area in the shape of a sector of a circle of radius 15 m.

sensor

15 m   15 m

The area of the sector is 200 square metres.

Find the length of the arc of the sector.

RA **4**

11. A cable car is used to carry sightseers up a mountain.

For safety reasons, the cable car company must consider the total weight of sightseers in a cable car.

They assume the average weight of an adult is 75 kilograms and the average weight of a child is 35 kilograms.

(a) Write down a formula for the **total** weight, W kilograms, of x adults and y children.

RA **2**

(b) In the busy season, the company sets the following conditions.

(i) **10** passengers must be carried at any one time.

(ii) Every child must be accompanied by **at least** one adult.

(iii) The maximum total weight which can be carried is 700 kilograms.

List all the combinations of adults and children which can now be carried in the cable car to meet all the above conditions.

Show all your working clearly.

RA **4**

12. The number of letters, N, which can be typed on a sheet of paper varies inversely as the square of the size, s, of the letters used.

(a) Write down a relationship connecting N and s.

KU **1**

(b) The size of the letters used is doubled.

What effect does this have on the number of letters which can be typed on the sheet of paper?

KU **2**

13. The diagram shows the positions of an oilrig and two ships.

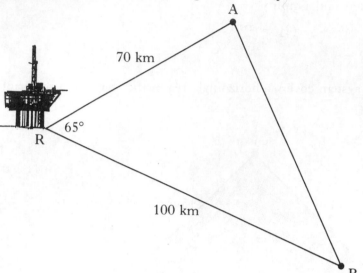

The oilrig at R is 70 kilometres from a ship at A and 100 kilometres from a ship at B. Angle ARB = 65°.

Calculate the distance AB.

Do not use a scale drawing.

4

14. A bottle bank is prism shaped, as shown in figure 1.

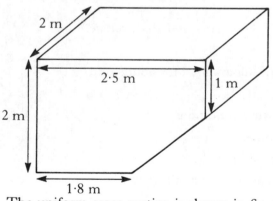

figure 1

The uniform cross-section is shown in figure 2.

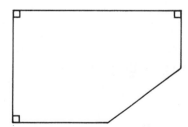

figure 2

Find the volume of the bottle bank.

4

16

KU	RA

15. A large floor is to be covered with black and grey square tiles to make a chequered pattern.

The person laying the tiles must start at the centre of the floor and work outwards.

The instructions are as follows.

1. **Lay a grey tile in the centre of the floor.**

1st Arrangement

2. **Place black tiles against the edges of the grey tile.**

2nd Arrangement

3. **Place grey tiles against the edges of all the black tiles.**

3rd Arrangement

4. **Place black tiles against the edges of all the grey tiles.**

5. **And so on . . .**

(a) How many tiles are there in the 4th arrangement?

(b) The number of tiles, T, needed to make the Nth arrangement is given by the formula

$$T = 2N^2 + aN + b.$$

Find the values of a and b.

KU	RA
	2
	4

16. A family want to build an extension at the rear of their house.

	KU	RA

width   length

An architect advises that the extension should have its length 2 metres more than its width.

(a) If the width of the extension is w metres, write down an expression for its length.

Planning regulations state that the area of the ground floor of the extension must not exceed 40% of the area of the ground floor of the original house.

(b) The ground floor of the original house is 12 metres by 10 metres.

Show that, if the largest extension is to be built, $w^2 + 2w - 48 = 0$.

(c) Find the dimensions of the largest extension which can be built.

17. Solve the equation

$$5 \sin x° + 2 = 0, \quad \text{for } 0 \leqslant x < 360.$$

18. (a) Express as a single fraction in its simplest form

$$\frac{3}{x} + \frac{2-x}{x^2}, \quad x \neq 0.$$

(b) Express $\dfrac{3}{\sqrt{5}}$ as a fraction with a rational denominator.

KU marks: 1 (16a), 3 (17), 3 (18a)
RA marks: 3 (16b), 2 (16c), 2 (18b)

19. Part of the graph of $y = x^3 - 3x + 1$ is shown in the diagram.

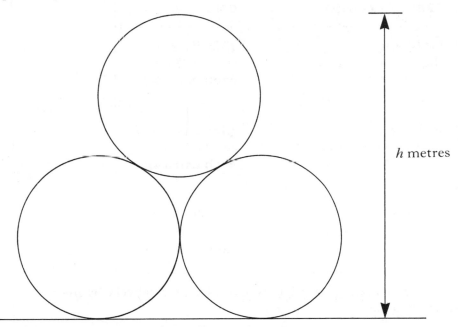

Use iteration to find the value of the **negative** root of $x^3 - 3x + 1 = 0$, correct to one decimal place.

Show all your working clearly.

4

20. Three pipes are stored on horizontal ground as shown in the diagram.

h metres

Each pipe has a circular cross-section with radius 1 metre.

Calculate the height, h metres, of the stacked pipes. **(Ignore the thickness of the pipes.)**

Give your answer in metres correct, to two decimal places.

4

[END OF QUESTION PAPER]

KU	RA

SCOTTISH
CERTIFICATE OF
EDUCATION
1995

FRIDAY, 5 MAY
1.30 PM – 3.45 PM

MATHEMATICS
STANDARD GRADE
Credit Level

	KU	RA

1. Solve the equation

$$5 - 2(1 + 3x) = 27.$$

KU: 3

2. Large distances in space are measured in light years.

A camera on a space telescope photographs a galaxy, a distance of 50 million light years away.

One light year is approximately $9 \cdot 46 \times 10^{12}$ kilometres.

Calculate the distance of the galaxy from the space telescope in kilometres.

Give your answer in scientific notation.

RA: 2

3. The cost of sending a parcel depends on the weight of the parcel and the time of delivery.

The cost is calculated as shown below.

TIME OF DELIVERY	COST
by 10 am the next working day	£**18·20** for 10 kg and £0·85 for **each extra kg.**
by noon the next working day	£**13·50** for 10 kg and £0·75 for **each extra kg.**
by 5pm the next working day	£**10·50** for 10 kg and £0·50 for **each extra kg.**

(a) Find the cost of sending a parcel, of weight 14 kg, for delivery **by noon** the next working day.

RA: 2

(b) Write down a formula to find the cost, £C, of sending a parcel, of weight w kg, where w is greater than 10.

The parcel has to be delivered **by noon** the next working day.

RA: 3

4. The Brown family want to convert the roof space in their bungalow into an extra room.

The roof space, with some of its measurements, is shown in figure 1.

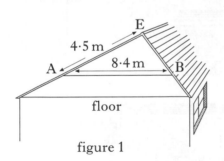

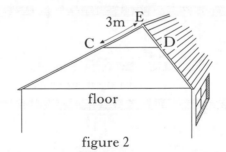

figure 1   figure 2

The position, AB, of the wooden beam must be changed to position CD, as shown in figure 2.

The wooden beam must always **be parallel to the floor**.

By considering the similar triangles EAB and ECD, calculate the length of the wooden beam in position CD.

Do not use a scale drawing.

3

5. The opening on this box of tissues is in the shape of an ellipse.

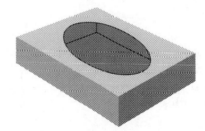

The graphs of two ellipses and their equations are shown below.

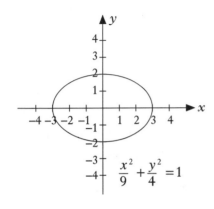

$$\frac{x^2}{9} + \frac{y^2}{4} = 1$$

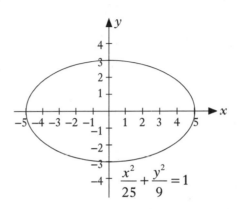

$$\frac{x^2}{25} + \frac{y^2}{9} = 1$$

Sketch the ellipse with equation

$$\frac{x^2}{36} + \frac{y^2}{16} = 1.$$

3

KU	RA

6. Ground has to be blasted and removed so that a motorway can be widened. The existing motorway and the motorway after widening are shown below.

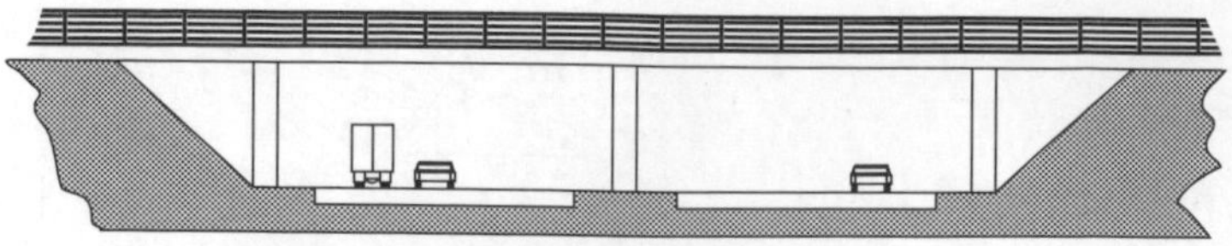

Existing motorway

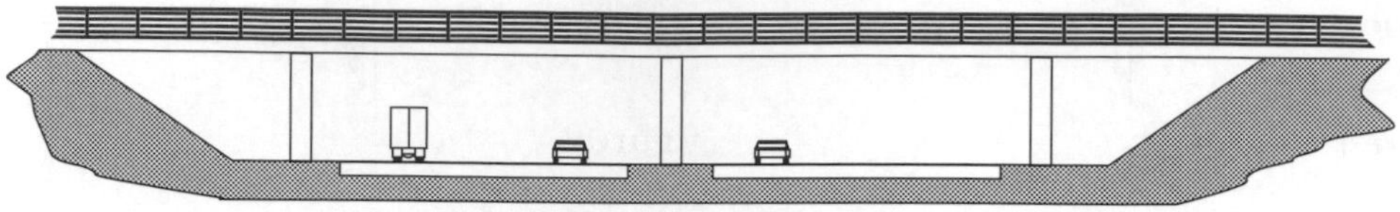

Motorway after widening

The uniform cross-section of the existing motorway consists of a rectangle and two congruent right-angled triangles as shown in figure 1.

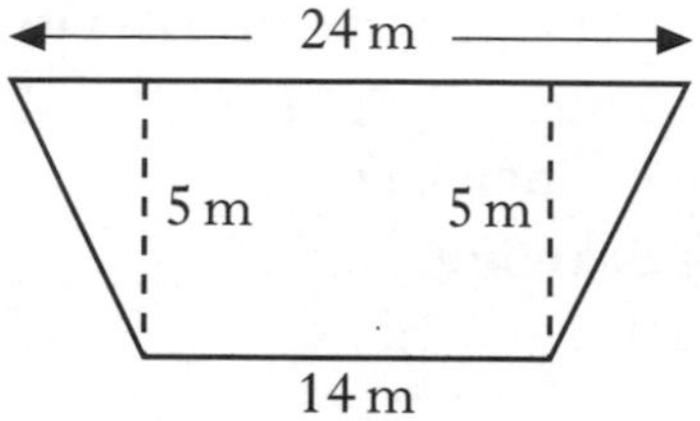

24 m

5 m   5 m

14 m

figure 1

The uniform cross-section of the motorway after widening consists of a rectangle and two congruent right-angled triangles as shown in figure 2.

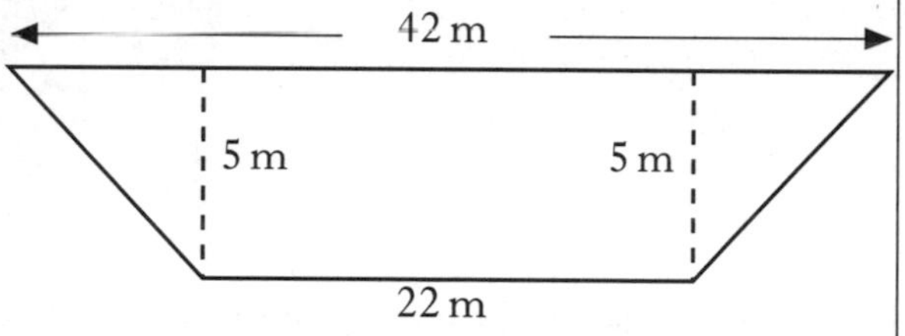

42 m

5 m   5 m

22 m

figure 2

The cost of blasting and removing each cubic metre of ground is £4.
10 kilometres of existing motorway is to be widened.
Find the total cost of blasting and removing the ground.

KU	RA
	4

7. A tank contains 10 litres of water.

A further 30 litres of water is poured into the tank at a steady rate of 5 litres per minute.

(*a*) On the 2 mm square-ruled graph paper provided, draw a graph of the volume, *V* litres, of water in the tank against the time, *t* minutes.

(*b*) Write down an equation connecting *V* and *t*.

8. The table shows the emission levels of harmful gases at different places in a city.

Emission Levels

City Sq	111 units
Albert Sq	41 units
Wellgate Centre	161 units
Bus Station	146 units
High St	114 units

Health regulations state that the emission levels of harmful gases should be **less** than 135 units.

The city council plan to reduce the levels in such a way that for each of the next 3 years the emission levels will be 5% less than the level in the previous year.

Will all the places listed in the table meet the health regulations in 3 years time?

Show clearly all your working.

KU: 4, 2

RA: 4

9. A field, ABC, is shown below.

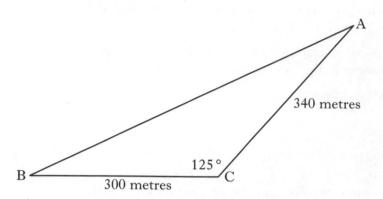

Find the area of the field.

KU RA

2

10. Brackets can be multiplied out in the following way.

$$(y+1)(y+2)(y+3) = y^3 + (1+2+3)y^2 + (1\times2+1\times3+2\times3)y + 1\times2\times3$$

$$(y+2)(y+3)(y+4) = y^3 + (2+3+4)y^2 + (2\times3+2\times4+3\times4)y + 2\times3\times4$$

$$(y+3)(y+4)(y+5) = y^3 + (3+4+5)y^2 + (3\times4+3\times5+4\times5)y + 3\times4\times5$$

(*a*) In the same way, multiply out

$$(y+4)(y+5)(y+6).$$

2

(*b*) In the same way, multiply out

$$(y+a)(y+b)(y+c).$$

2

	KU	RA

11. (a) $f(x) = 3\sqrt{x}$

Find the exact value of $f(12)$, giving your answer as a **surd, in its simplest form**.

KU: 2

(b) Express $\dfrac{y^4 \times y}{y^{-2}}$ in its simplest form.

KU: 2

(c) Factorise $9a^2 - 25$.

KU: 2

12.

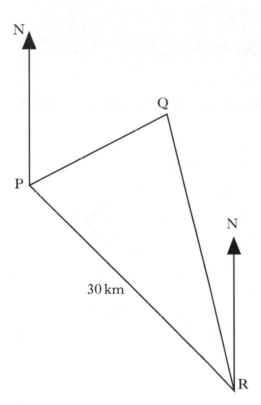

30 km

A ship, at position P, observes a lighthouse at position Q on a bearing of 040°.

The ship travels 30 kilometres on a bearing of 125° to position R.

From position R, the ship observes the lighthouse on a bearing of 340°.

When the ship is at position R, how far is it from the lighthouse?

RA: 6

13. Solve the equation

$$x^2 + 2x - 6 = 0.$$

Give your answers correct to 2 significant figures.

KU   RA

5

14. Figure 1 shows a road bridge.

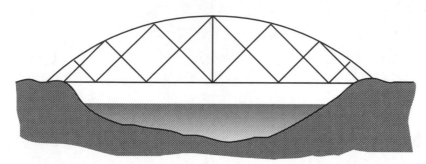

figure 1

The curved part of the bridge is formed from an arc of a circle, centre O, as shown in figure 2.

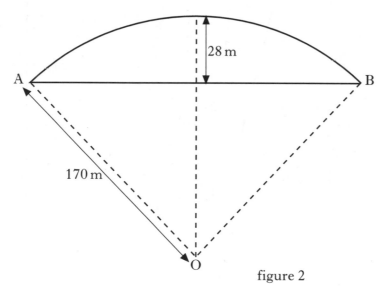

figure 2

OA and OB are radii of length 170 metres.

The height of the middle of the bridge above its ends is 28 metres as shown in figure 2.

Calculate the horizontal distance, AB.

Do not use a scale drawing.

4

	KU	RA

15. Alloys are made by mixing metals.

Two different alloys are made using iron and lead.

To make the first alloy, 3 cubic centimetres of iron and 4 cubic centimetres of lead are used.

This alloy weighs 65 grams.

(a) Let x grams be the weight of 1 cubic centimetre of iron and y grams be the weight of 1 cubic centimetre of lead.

Write down an equation in x and y which satisfies the above condition.   **2**

To make the second alloy, 5 cubic centimetres of iron and 7 cubic centimetres of lead are used.

This alloy weighs 112 grams.

(b) Write down a second equation in x and y which satisfies this condition.   **2**

(c) Find the weight of 1 cubic centimetre of iron and the weight of 1 cubic centimetre of lead.   **3**

16. $M = R^2 t - 3$

Change the subject of the formula to R.   **3**

17.

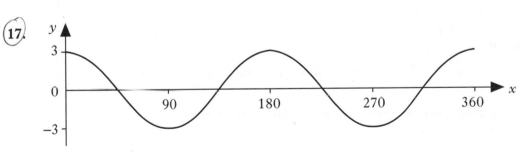

The diagram shows the graph of $y = a\cos bx°$, $0 \le x < 360$.

Find the values of a and b.   **2**

18. A table of pairs of values of x and y is shown below.

x	1·5	2	2·5
y	6	4·5	3·6

(a)   Explain why y varies inversely as x.

(b)   Write down the formula connecting x and y.

19.   Pipes with equal diameters are arranged in a stack.

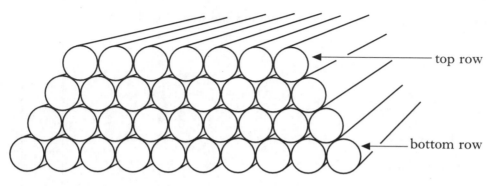

top row

bottom row

To find the number of pipes, P, in a stack, the following formula can be used

$$P = \frac{(b+a)\,(b-a+1)}{2}$$

where b is the number of pipes on the bottom row and a is the number of pipes on the top row.

(a)   Use this formula to find the number of pipes in a stack where $b = 40$ and $a = 15$.

(b)   In a particular stack, the number of pipes on the bottom row is twice the number on the top row.

Show that in this stack $P = \frac{3a^2 + 3a}{2}$, where a is the number of pipes on the top row.

(c)   Would it be possible to arrange exactly 975 pipes in the kind of stack described in part (b) ?

Justify your answer.

[END OF QUESTION PAPER]

SCOTTISH
CERTIFICATE OF
EDUCATION
1996

THURSDAY, 9 MAY
1.30 PM – 3.45 PM

MATHEMATICS
STANDARD GRADE
Credit Level

KU	RA

1. Solve **algebraically** the inequality

$$2 + 5x \geq 8x - 16.$$

3

2. A ramp is being made from concrete.

The uniform cross-section of the ramp consists of a right-angled triangle and a rectangle as shaded in the diagram below.

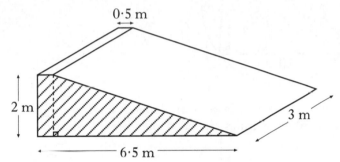

Find the volume of concrete required to make the ramp.

2

3. The boat on a carnival ride travels along an arc of a circle, centre C.

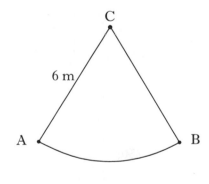

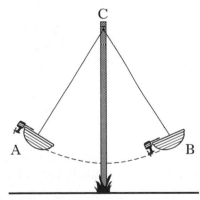

The boat is attached to C by a rod 6 metres long.

The rod swings from position CA to position CB.

The length of the arc AB is 7 metres.

Find the angle through which the rod swings from position A to position B.

4

4. The area, A, of a quadrilateral drawn inside a circle can be found using the formula

$$A = \sqrt{(s-a)(s-b)(s-c)(s-d)},$$

where $s = \dfrac{(a+b+c+d)}{2}$.

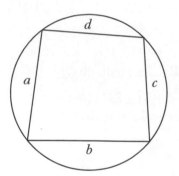

Use this formula to find the area of the quadrilateral shown in the diagram below. **Give your answer correct to 2 significant figures.**

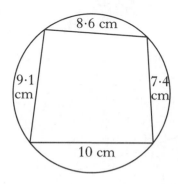

5. The travelling expenses claimed by a salesperson depend on the engine capacity of the car and the number of miles travelled per week as shown in the table below.

ENGINE CAPACITY	EXPENSES PER MILE
less than or equal to 1 litre	£0·25 for **each** of the first 250 miles travelled
greater than 1 litre but **less than or equal to** 1·2 litres	£0·27 for **each** of the first 250 miles travelled
greater than 1·2 litres	£0·29 for **each** of the first 250 miles travelled

Where the number of miles travelled in a week **is greater than 250**, £0·15 can be claimed for **each additional** mile.

(a) Find the expenses claimed by a salesperson in a week when 550 miles are travelled and the engine capacity is 1·6 litres.

(b) Write down a formula to find the expenses, £E, claimed for t miles travelled, where t is greater than 250, and the engine capacity is 1·6 litres.

KU	RA
	3
	2
	3

6. The surface area of a planet, A square kilometres, varies directly as the square of the diameter, D kilometres, of the planet.

The surface area of the Moon is $3 \cdot 8 \times 10^7$ square kilometres.

Calculate the surface area of a planet with diameter double the diameter of the Moon.

Give your answer in scientific notation.

7. The graph shows the volume of petrol in a car's tank during a journey.

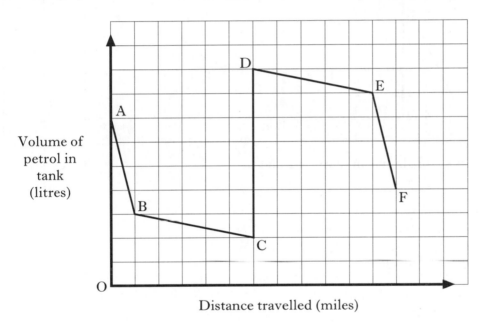

Distance travelled (miles)

(*a*) Explain the significance of CD.

The journey involves driving through towns and along motorways.

In the towns the car uses more petrol per mile than on the motorways.

(*b*) Which **two** parts of the graph show driving on motorways?

Explain your answer clearly.

KU	RA
3	
1	
	2

8.

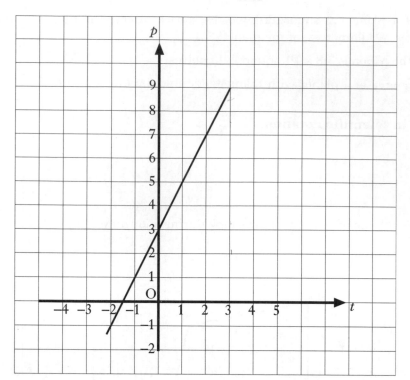

Find the equation of the straight line in terms of p and t.

KU | RA

4

9. The side wall of a house, with measurements as shown below, requires painting.

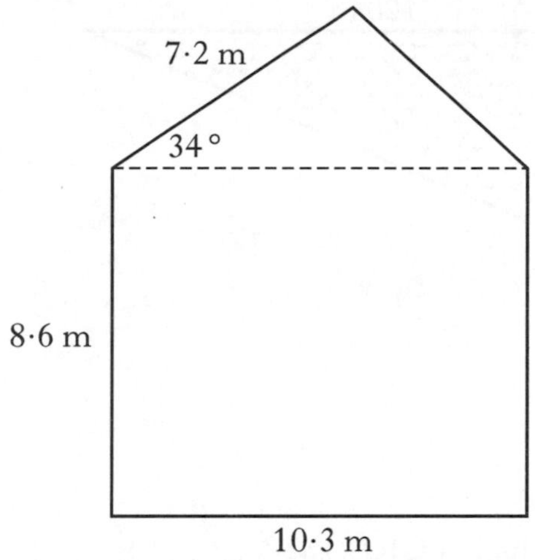

7·2 m

34°

8·6 m

10·3 m

The wall is in the shape of a rectangle and a triangle.

On average, a litre of paint will cover 8 square metres.

A painter estimates that he will require 12 litres of paint.

Will this be enough paint?

Justify your answer.

KU | RA

4

10. (a) Factorise $3x^2 - 5x - 2$.

(b) Solve **algebraically** the equation

$$\frac{m}{3} = \frac{(1-m)}{5}.$$

(c) Solve **algebraically** the equation

$$6y - y^2 = 0.$$

2

3

2

11. A triangular field, PQR, is shown below.

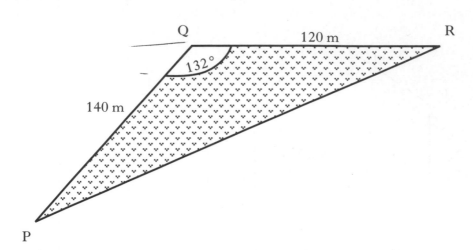

PQ = 140 metres, QR = 120 metres and angle PQR = 132°.

Calculate the length of PR.

Do not use a scale drawing.

4

12. In 1995, the price of 1 litre of a certain kind of petrol was 54·9 pence.

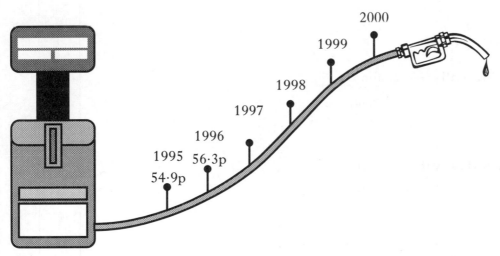

By 1996, the price of 1 litre of the same kind of petrol had risen to 56·3 pence.

The percentage increase for each of the next four years is expected to be the same as the percentage increase between 1995 and 1996.

What is the price of 1 litre of petrol expected to be in the year 2000?

4

13. Solve **algebraically** the equation

$$5 \tan x° - 9 = 0, \text{ for } 0 \leq x < 360.$$

KU 3

14. The integral part of a positive real number is the part of the number which is an integer.

EXAMPLES: **The integral part of 5·6 is 5.**
This can be written as **[5·6] = 5**.

The integral part of 6·2 is 6.
This can be written as **[6·2] = 6**.

(*a*) Find [16·7].

RA 1

(*b*) Identical boxes are packed on a board for storage.

The boxes are all packed the same way round (two boxes are shown in the diagram).

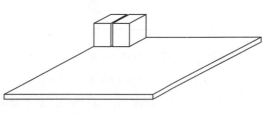

(i)

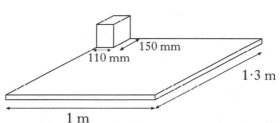

The base of each box measures 150 millimetres by 110 millimetres. The board measures 1·3 metres by 1 metre.

The number of boxes which can fit along the 1·3 metre length is given by $\left[\dfrac{1300}{150}\right]$.

Find $\left[\dfrac{1300}{150}\right]$.

RA 1

(ii) Write down an expression for the number of boxes which can be packed on the board shown below.

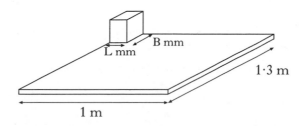

RA 2

15. The diagram shows two positions of a student as she views the top of a tower.

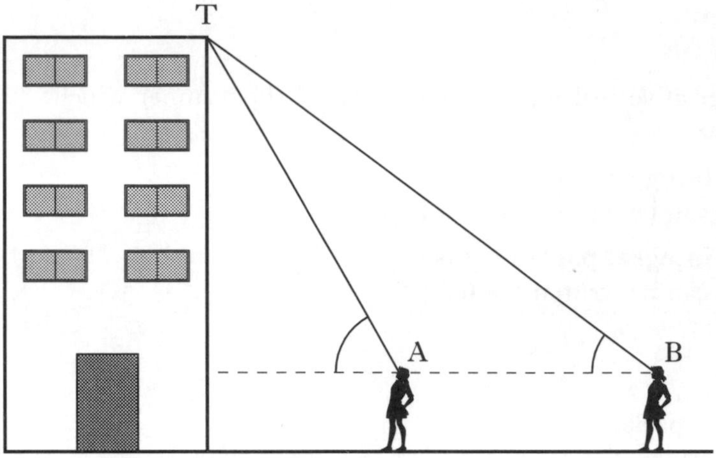

From position B, the angle of elevation to T at the top of the tower is $64°$.

From position A, the angle of elevation to T at the top of the tower is $69°$.

The distance AB is $4\cdot8$ metres and the height of the student to eye level is $1\cdot5$ metres.

Find the height of the tower.

16. (a) Remove the brackets and simplify

$$b^{\frac{1}{2}}(b^{\frac{1}{2}} + b^{-\frac{1}{2}}).$$

(b) $f(x) = \dfrac{3}{\sqrt{x}}$

Find the **exact** value of $f(2)$.

Give your answer **as a fraction** with a rational denominator.

(c) $Q = p^2 + 3T$

Change the subject of the formula to T.

	KU	RA
15.		6
16.(a)	3	
(b)	2	
(c)	2	

17. A sequence of numbers is

1, 5, 12, 22, ...

Numbers from this sequence can be illustrated in the following way using dots.

First Number
  (N = 1)

Second Number
  (N = 2)

Third Number
  (N = 3)

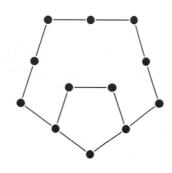

Fourth Number
  (N = 4)

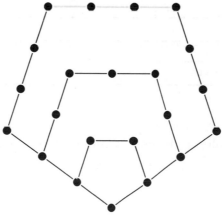

(*a*) What is the fifth number in this sequence?

Illustrate this in a sketch.

(*b*) The number of dots, D, needed to illustrate the Nth number in this sequence is given by the formula

$$D = aN^2 - bN.$$

Find the values of a and b.

KU	RA
	2
	4

18. (a) The equation $x^3 + 2x^2 - 5 = 0$ has a root between 1 and 2.

Use iteration to find the value of this root correct to one decimal place.

Show clearly all your working.

KU 3

(b) Express as a single fraction in its simplest form

$$\frac{5}{x} - \frac{3}{(x-2)}, \quad x \neq 0 \quad \text{or} \quad x \neq 2.$$

KU 3

19. A rectangular sheet of plastic 18 cm by 100 cm is used to make a gutter for draining rain water.

The gutter is made by bending the sheet of plastic as shown below in diagram 1.

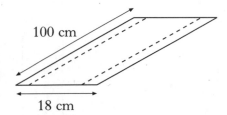

100 cm

18 cm

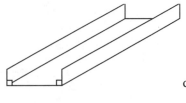

diagram 1

(a) The depth of the gutter is x centimetres as shown in diagram 2 below. Write down an expression in x for the width of the gutter.

RA 1

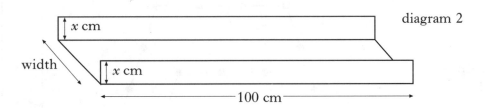

diagram 2

x cm

width

x cm

100 cm

(b) Show that the volume, V cubic centimetres, of this gutter is given by
$$V = 1800x - 200x^2.$$

RA 2

(c) Find the dimensions of the gutter which has the largest volume.

Show clearly all your working.

RA 4

[END OF QUESTION PAPER]

SCOTTISH
CERTIFICATE OF
EDUCATION
1997

FRIDAY, 9 MAY
1.15 PM – 3.30 PM

MATHEMATICS
STANDARD GRADE
Credit Level

1.

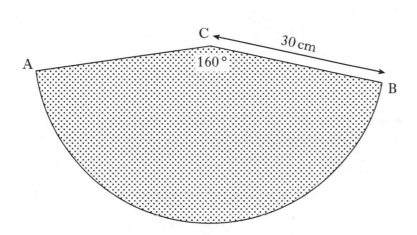

The diagram shows a sector of a circle, centre C.

Angle ACB is 160° and the radius of the circle is 30 cm.

Calculate the length of the arc AB.

KU	RA
3	

2. A storage barn is prism shaped, as shown below.

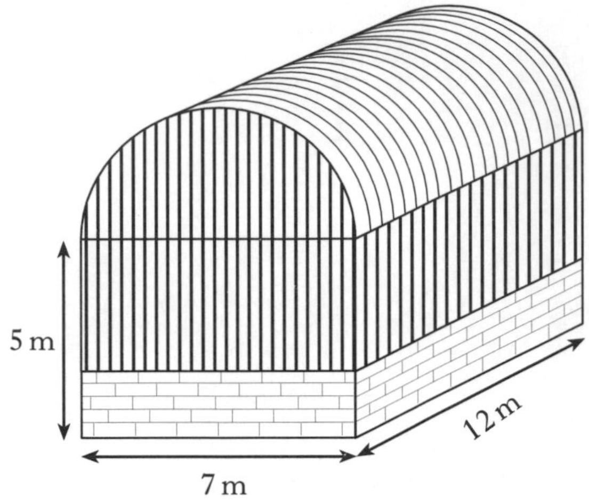

The cross-section of the storage barn consists of a rectangle measuring 7 metres by 5 metres and a semi-circle of radius 3·5 metres.

(*a*) Find the volume of the storage barn.

Give your answer in cubic metres, **correct to 2 significant figures**.

4

(*b*) An extension to the barn is planned to increase the volume by 200 cubic metres.

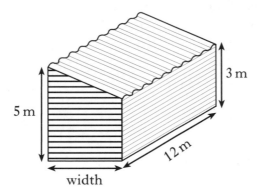

The uniform cross-section of the extension consists of a rectangle and a right-angled triangle.

Find the width of the extension.

3

3. While on holiday, John's family decide to hire a car.

There are two different schemes for hiring the same type of car, Eurocar and Apex.

<table>
<tr><td>

EUROCAR HIRE

No deposit required
£15 per day

</td><td>

APEX HIRE

£50 deposit required
plus
£10 per day

</td></tr>
</table>

(a) Write down a formula to find the cost, £C, of hiring the car from Eurocar for d days.

1

(b) Write down a formula to find the cost, £C, of hiring the car from Apex for d days.

2

(c) John's family have £170 to spend on car hire.

Which scheme should they use to have the car for as long as possible?

Show clearly all your working.

4

4. The sketch below shows a plot of ground, PQRS, split into two triangles.

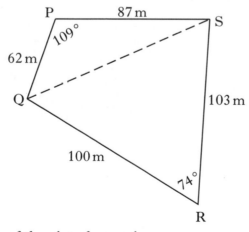

Calculate the area of the plot of ground.

4

5. On a £500 holiday, a company offers an easy payment scheme.

£100 is repaid on the 15th of each month.

Interest is charged at a rate of 2·5% per month on the amount outstanding **at the end** of each month.

The first payment is to be made in May.

Find the amount outstanding at the beginning of August.

3

6. The diagram shows the design of an earring.

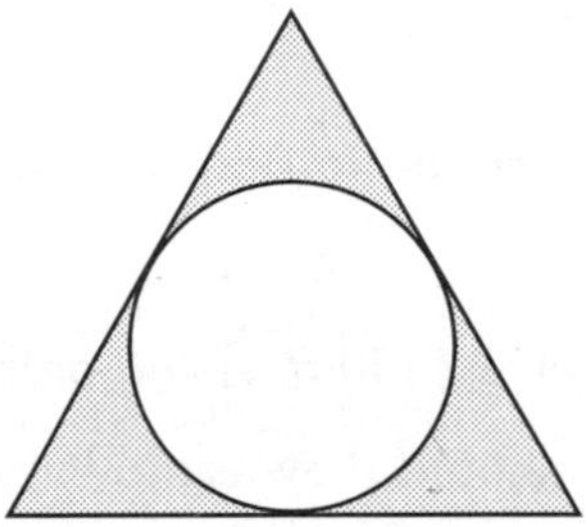

The earring consists of a circle placed inside an equilateral triangle.

The sides of the triangle are tangents to the circle.

The radius of the circle is 8 mm.

The distance from the centre of the circle to **each** vertex of the triangle is 17 mm.

Calculate the perimeter of the triangle.

4

7. Figure 1 shows part of the street plan of a town.

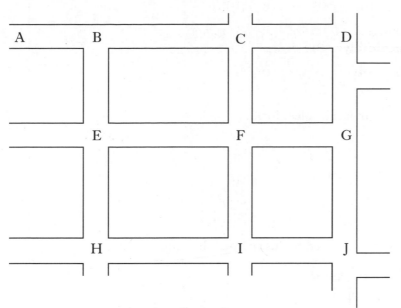

figure 1

Vehicles can travel in both directions along each street.

As a vehicle travels on the straight parts of any street it can reach the maximum speed.

The speed is always reduced on the bends.

The graph in figure 2 shows how the speed of a vehicle changes as it travels from **A to J**.

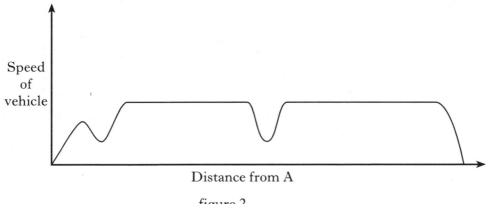

figure 2

(a) What route did the vehicle travel? Use the letters from figure 1 to indicate this route.

(b) Another vehicle took the route A, B, C, F, G and J.

Sketch a graph to show how the speed of this vehicle changes during the journey.

2

3

8. (a) $h(t) = 15t - 3t^2$

Find $h(-2)$.

(b) (i) Factorise **completely**

$$2x^2 - 6x.$$

(ii) Express $\dfrac{2x^2 - 6x}{x^2 - 9}$ in its simplest form.

9. Consecutive cubic numbers can be added using the following pattern.

$$1^3 + 2^3 \qquad = \frac{2^2 \times 3^2}{4}$$

$$1^3 + 2^3 + 3^3 \qquad = \frac{3^2 \times 4^2}{4}$$

$$1^3 + 2^3 + 3^3 + 4^3 \qquad = \frac{4^2 \times 5^2}{4}$$

(a) Express $1^3 + 2^3 + 3^3 + 4^3 + 5^3 + 6^3 + 7^3$ in the same way.

(b) Write down an expression for the sum of the first n consecutive cubic numbers.

(c) Write down an expression for $8^3 + 9^3 + 10^3 + \ldots + n^3$.

KU	RA
2	
1	
2	
	2
	3
	2

10. The number of litres of petrol, L, used by a car on a journey varies directly as the distance travelled, D kilometres, and as the square root of the average speed, S kilometres per hour.

(a) Write down a relationship connecting L, D and S.

	KU	RA
	1	

The car uses 30 litres of petrol for a journey of 550 kilometres when it travels at an average speed of 81 kilometres per hour.

(b) How many litres of petrol does the car use for a journey of 693 kilometres travelling at an average speed of 100 kilometres per hour?

3

11. (a) Remove the brackets and collect like terms

$$(3a - b)(2a - 5b).$$

2

(b) Solve **algebraically** the equation

$$2x^2 - 9x - 5 = 0.$$

3

(c) Solve **algebraically** the equation

$$\frac{x}{2} - \frac{(x + 1)}{3} = 4.$$

3

12. The diagram shows the positions of three airports, A, E and G.

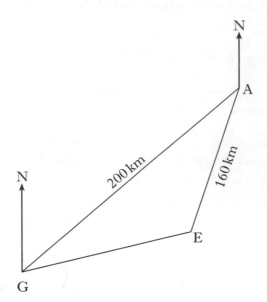

G is 200 kilometres from A.

E is 160 kilometres from A.

From G the bearing of A is 052°.

From A the bearing of E is 216°.

How far apart are airports G and E?

6

13.

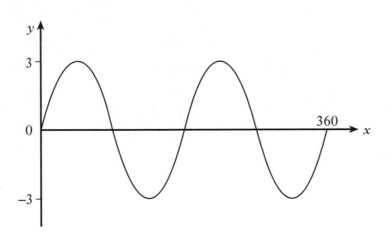

The diagram shows the graph of $y = k\sin ax°$, $0 \le x < 360$.

Find the values of a and k.

2

KU	RA

14. A number tower is built from bricks as shown in figure 1.

The number on the brick above is always equal to the sum of the two numbers below.

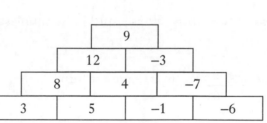

figure 1

(a) Find the number on the shaded brick in figure 2.

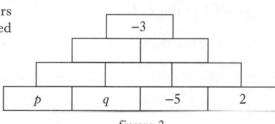

figure 2

(b) In figure 3, two of the numbers on the base bricks are represented by p and q.

Show that $p + 3q = 10$.

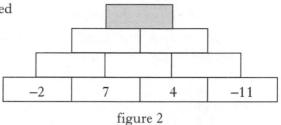

figure 3

(c) Use figure 4 to write down a second equation in p and q.

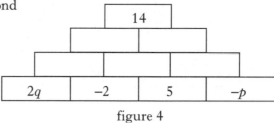

figure 4

(d) Find the values of p and q.

KU	RA
1	
	2
	2
	3

	KU	RA

15. (a) Express $\sqrt{72} - \sqrt{2} + \sqrt{50}$ as a surd in its simplest form. — 3

(b) Express $\dfrac{3y^5 \times 4y^{-1}}{6y}$ in its simplest form. — 3

16. A toy is hanging by a spring from the ceiling.

Once the toy is set moving, the height, H metres, of the toy above the floor is given by the formula

$$H = 1\cdot9 + 0\cdot3\cos(30t)°$$

t seconds after starting to move.

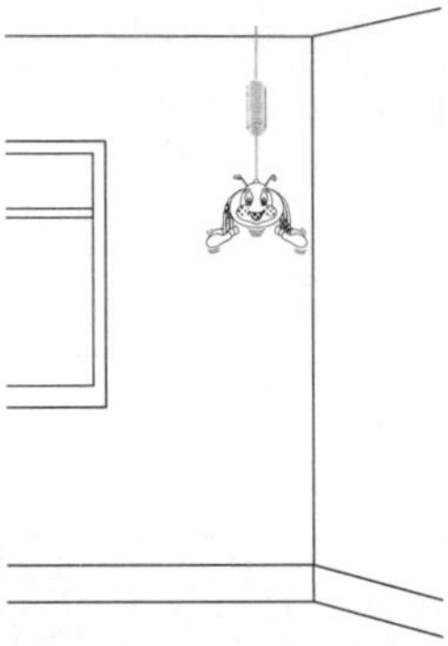

(a) State the maximum value of H. — 1

(b) Calculate the height of the toy above the floor after 8 seconds. — 3

(c) When is the height of the toy **first** 2·05 metres above the floor? — 3

[END OF QUESTION PAPER]

SCOTTISH
CERTIFICATE OF
EDUCATION
1998

FRIDAY, 8 MAY
1.20 PM – 3.35 PM

MATHEMATICS
STANDARD GRADE
Credit Level

	KU	RA

1. The annual profit (£) of a company was $3 \cdot 2 \times 10^9$ for the year 1997.

What profit did the company make per second?

Give your answer to **three significant figures**.

KU: 2

2. Two parachutists, X and Y, jump from two separate aircrafts at different times.

The graph shows how their height above the ground changes over a period of time.

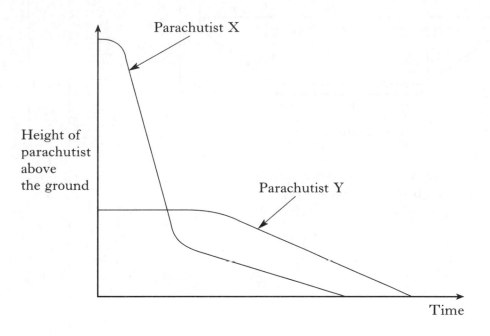

(a) Which parachutist jumped first?

RA: 1

(b) Which parachutist did not open his parachute immediately after jumping?

Explain your answer clearly.

RA: 2

3. A skip is prism shaped as shown in figure 1.

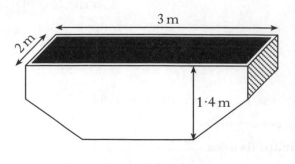

figure 1

The cross-section of the skip, with measurements in metres, is shown in figure 2.

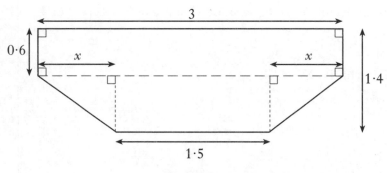

figure 2

(*a*) Find the value of x.

(*b*) Find the volume of the skip in cubic metres.

KU	RA
	1
	3

4. A sequence of terms, starting with 1, is

1, 5, 9, 13, 17, ...

Consecutive terms in this sequence are formed by adding 4 to the previous term.

The total of consecutive terms of this sequence can be found using the following pattern.

Total of the first 2 terms: $1 + 5$ $= 2 \times 3$
Total of the first 3 terms: $1 + 5 + 9$ $= 3 \times 5$
Total of the first 4 terms: $1 + 5 + 9 + 13$ $= 4 \times 7$
Total of the first 5 terms: $1 + 5 + 9 + 13 + 17 = 5 \times 9$

(a) Express the total of the first 9 terms of this sequence in the same way.

(b) The first n terms of this sequence are added. Write down an expression, in n, for the total.

5.

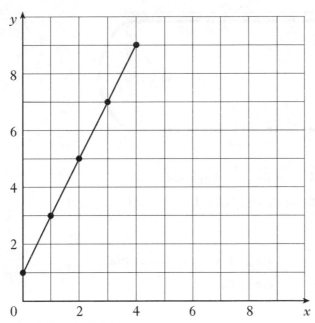

Find the equation of the straight line.

KU	RA
	2
	3
3	

6. Triangles ABE and ACD, with some of their measurements, are shown opposite.

Triangle ABE is similar to triangle ACD.

Calculate the length of BE.

Do not use a scale drawing.

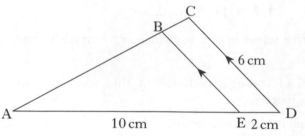

7. The diagram below shows a ceiling in the shape of a rectangle and a segment of a circle.

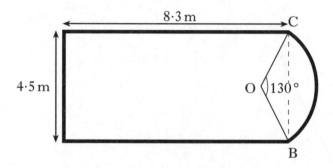

The rectangle measures 8·3 metres by 4·5 metres.

OB and OC are radii of the circle and angle BOC is 130°.

(*a*) Find the length of OB.

A border has to be fitted round the perimeter of the ceiling.

(*b*) Find the length of border required.

KU	RA
3	
	3
	4

8. Figure 1 shows the circular cross-section of a tunnel with a horizontal floor.

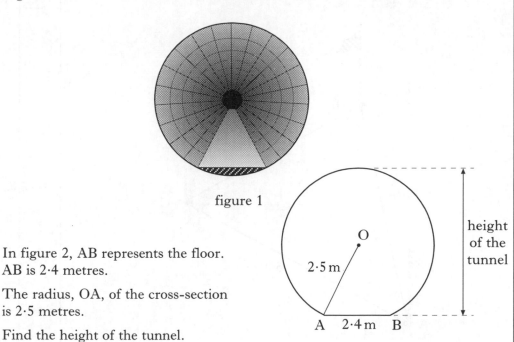

figure 1

In figure 2, AB represents the floor. AB is 2·4 metres.

The radius, OA, of the cross-section is 2·5 metres.

Find the height of the tunnel.

figure 2

4

9. The cost of taking a school group to the theatre can be calculated from the information shown below.

* 1 adult goes free for every 10 pupils *

Number of pupils	Cost per pupil	Cost per paying adult
less than 10	£5·00	£8·00
10 to 19	£4·50	£7·00
20 to 29	£4·00	£6·00
30 to 39	£3·00	£5·00

(a) Find the cost for a group of 12 pupils and 3 adults.

2

(b) Write down a formula to find the cost, £C, of taking a group of p pupils and d adults where $20 \leq p \leq 29$.

4

10. The diagram shows part of a golf course.

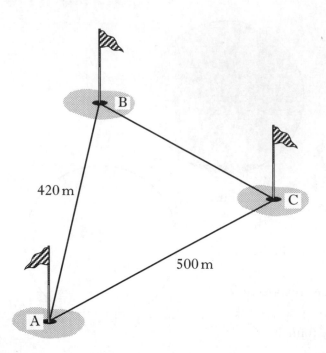

The distance AB is 420 metres, the distance AC is 500 metres and angle BAC = 52°.

Calculate the distance BC.

Do not use a scale drawing.

KU | RA

3

11. (*a*) Solve, **algebraically**, the system of equations

$$2a + 4b = -7$$
$$3a - 5b = 17.$$

3

(*b*) Change the subject of the formula to k

$$d = \frac{k - m}{t}.$$

2

(*c*) Solve, **algebraically**, the equation

$$x^2 = 7x.$$

3

12. An aeroplane is flying parallel to the ground.

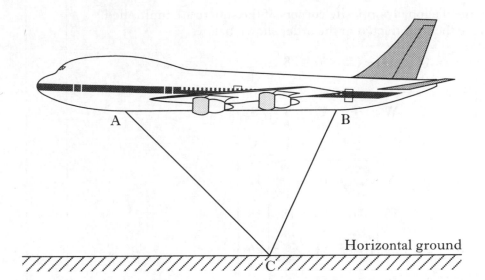

	KU	RA

Lights have been fitted at A and B as shown in the diagram.

When the aeroplane is flying at a certain height, the beams from these lights meet exactly on the ground at C.

The angle of depression of the beam of light from A to C is 50°.

The angle of depression of the beam of light from B to C is 70°.

The distance AB is 20 metres.

Find the height of the aeroplane above C.

6

13. The time, T minutes, taken for a stadium to empty varies directly as the number of spectators, S, and inversely as the number of open exits, E.

(*a*) Write down a relationship connecting T, S and E.

1

It takes 12 minutes for a stadium to empty when there are 20 000 spectators and 20 open exits.

(*b*) How long does it take the stadium to empty when there are 36 000 spectators and 24 open exits?

3

14. A 3×3 square has been identified on the calendar below.

The numbers in the diagonally opposite corners of the square are multiplied. These products are then subtracted in the order shown below.

$$(23 \times 11) - (25 \times 9) = 28$$

M	T	W	T	F	S	S
		1	2	3	4	5
6	7	8	9	10	11	12
13	14	15	16	17	18	19
20	21	22	23	24	25	26
27	28	29	30	31		

(*a*) Repeat the above process for a different 3×3 square.

Show clearly all your working.

(*b*) Prove that **in every** 3×3 square on the calendar above the process gives the answer 28.

15. Solve, **algebraically**, the equation

$$7\cos x° - 2 = 0, \quad \text{for } 0 \le x < 360.$$

16. Traffic authorities are investigating the number of cars travelling along a busy stretch of road.

They assume that all cars are travelling at a speed of v metres per second.

The number of cars, N, which pass a particular point on the road in one minute is given by the formula

$$N = \frac{30v}{2 + v}.$$

In one minute, 26 cars pass a point on the road.

Find the speed of the cars in metres per second.

KU | RA

1

3

3

3

	KU	RA

17. (a) Factorise $4a^2 - 9b^2$.   **2**

(b) Express as a single fraction in its simplest form

$$\frac{1}{2x} - \frac{1}{3x}, \quad x \neq 0.$$

     2

18. On a certain day the depth, D metres, of water at a fishing port, t hours after midnight, is given by the formula

$D = 12 \cdot 5 + 9 \cdot 5 \sin (30t)°.$

(a) Find the depth of the water at 1.30 pm.   **3**

(b) The depth of water in the harbour is recorded each hour. What is the maximum difference in the depths of water in the harbour over the 24 hour period?

Show clearly all your working.   **3**

19. (a) Multiply out the brackets

$$\sqrt{2}(\sqrt{6} - \sqrt{2}).$$

Express your answer as a **surd** in its simplest form.   **2**

(b) Express $\dfrac{b^{\frac{1}{2}} \times b^{\frac{3}{2}}}{b}$ in its simplest form.   **2**

[END OF QUESTION PAPER]

1. $18 \cdot 8$ m^2 2. $65 \cdot 6$ mg

3. 250 000   4. *(a)* £642   *(b)* $C = 29t + 149$

5. *(a)* Graph of volume against time   *(b)* $V = -20t + 240$

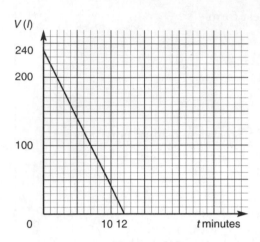

6. *(a)* $\dfrac{10 \times 11 \times 21}{6}$ *(b)* $\dfrac{n(n+1)(2n+1)}{6}$

7. $a = 3$; $b = -2$

8. *(a)* Proof {use the difference of two squares}

   (b) $x = 13$; $y = 11$

9. $0 \cdot 61$ litres

10. *(a)* $28 \cdot 3\%$ *(b)* $1 \cdot 8\%$

11. $59 \cdot 9$ m^2

12. *(a)* $1 : \sqrt{2}$ *(b)* Proof {use a square of side x cm}

13. *(a)* $T = \dfrac{4L}{\sqrt{H}}$ *(b)* $12 \cdot 5$ s

14. $15 \cdot 9$ m

15. *(a)* $15a^2 - 2ab - 8b^2$ *(b)* $x = -4$ or $\dfrac{3}{2}$

16. *(a)* $1 \cdot 25$ million gallons   *(b)* Yes: (during May and June)

17. *(a)* 8   *(b)* $6\sqrt{2}$

18. *(a)* (i) $12h$ minutes   (ii) $\dfrac{v}{10}$ minutes   (iii) Proof $\left\{ \dfrac{\text{(i) + (ii)}}{60} \right\}$

    (b) Yes: should finish return journey by 1742 hours

1. $a = 10$

2. Approx 14 million (13·8915 million)

3. YES; since the slope $= 26·6°$

4. *(a)* $b = 108$ *(b)* Proof {use corresponding then supplementary angles}

5. Proof {use the converse of Pythagoras}

6. *(a)* 12×14 *(b)* Total $= n^2 + 2n$

7. Speed $\doteqdot 18\,000$ kph

8. *(a)* Dipstick ②, since marks are closer at the bottom and further apart at the top, to allow for the shape of the tank.

(b)

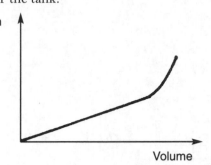

9. *(a)* $4y^2 - 12y + 9$ *(b)* $(2x - 1)(x + 4)$

10. Length $\doteqdot 26·7$ m

11. *(a)* $W = 75x + 35y$ *(b)*

Adults	Children
5	5
6	4
7	3
8	2

12. *(a)* $N = \dfrac{k}{s^2} \left\{ \text{or } N\alpha\dfrac{1}{s^2} \right\}$ *(b)* The number of letters is quartered.

13. AB $\doteqdot 94·8$ km

14. Volume $= 9·3$ m^3

15. *(a)* 25 tiles *(b)* $a = -2; \ b = 1$

16. *(a)* Length $= (w + 2)$ metres *(b)* Proof *(c)* Dimensions 6×8 metres

17. $x = 203·6°, \ 336·4°$

18. *(a)* $\dfrac{2x + 2}{x^2}$ *(b)* $\dfrac{3\sqrt{5}}{5}$

19. $x \doteqdot -1·9$

20. $h \doteqdot 3·73$

1. $x = -4$

2. $4 \cdot 73 \times 10^{20}$

3. *(a)* £16.50   *(b)* $C = 0 \cdot 75w + 6$

4. $5 \cdot 6$ m

5.

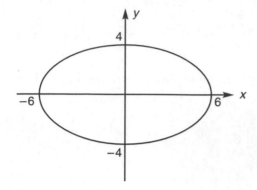

6. £2 600 000

7. *(a)*

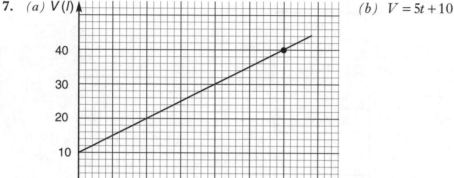

(b) $V = 5t + 10$

8. NO; (since Wellgate Centre will NOT)

9. Area $\doteqdot 41\ 800$ m^2

10. *(a)* $y^3 + 15y^2 + 74y + 120$ *(b)* $y^3 + (a + b + c)y^2 + (ab + ac + bc)y + abc$

11. *(a)* $6\sqrt{3}$ *(b)* y^7 *(c)* $(3a + 5)(3a - 5)$

12. $34 \cdot 5$ km

13. $-3 \cdot 6$ or $1 \cdot 6$

14. AB $= 186 \cdot 9$ m

15. *(a)* $3x + 4y = 65$ *(b)* $5x + 7y = 112$ *(c)* 1cc IRON weighs 7 g; 1 cc LEAD weighs 11 g

16. $R = \pm \sqrt{\left(\dfrac{M + 3}{t} \right)}$

17. $a = 3;\ b = 2$

18. *(a)* Since $xy = 9$ constant   *(b)* $y = \dfrac{9}{x}$

19. *(a)* $P = 715$ *(b)* Proof   *(c)* YES; (25 on top row and 50 on bottom row)

1. $x \leq 6$ **2.** $21\,\text{m}^3$ **3.** $66 \cdot 8°$ **4.** $76\,\text{cm}^2$

5. *(a)* £117.50   *(b)* $E = 0 \cdot 15t + 35$ **6.** $1 \cdot 52 \times 10^8$

7. *(a)* Tank was refilled   *(b)* BC and DE {the gradient is less}

8. $P = 2t + 3$ **9.** NO; {short by $1 \cdot 67\,l$}

10. *(a)* $(3x + 1)(x - 2)$ *(b)* $m = \dfrac{3}{8}$ {or $0 \cdot 375$}   *(c)* $y = 0$ or 6

11. $PR = 237 \cdot 7\,\text{m}$ **12.** $62 \cdot 3\text{p}$ per litre

13. $x = 60 \cdot 9$ or $240 \cdot 9$

14. *(a)* 16 *(b)* (i) 8 (ii) Number $= \left[\dfrac{1300}{B}\right] \times \left[\dfrac{1000}{L}\right]$

15. Height $\doteqdot 47 \cdot 7\,\text{m}$ **16.** *(a)* $b + 1$ *(b)* $\dfrac{3\sqrt{2}}{2}$ *(c)* $T = \dfrac{Q - p^2}{3}$

17. *(a)* 35 *(b)* $a = \dfrac{3}{2}$ $b = \dfrac{1}{2}$

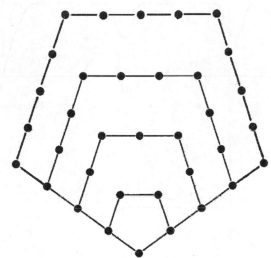

18. *(a)* Root is $x \doteqdot 1 \cdot 2$ *(b)* $\dfrac{2x - 10}{x(x - 2)}$

19. *(a)* $w = 18 - 2x\,\text{cm}$ *(b)* Proof {Hint use $V = l \times b \times h$. Here $V = l \times w \times d$}
    (c) Dimensions are $100\,\text{cm} \times 9\,\text{cm} \times 4 \cdot 5\,\text{cm}$

1. $AB \doteqdot 84$ cm

2. (a) 650 m^3 (b) $4 \cdot 2$ m

3. (a) $C = 15d$ (b) $C = 10d + 50$ (c) Apex Hire

4. Area $\doteqdot 7500$ m^2

5. £223.19

6. $P = 90$ mm

7. (a) A, B, E, H, I and J

   (b)

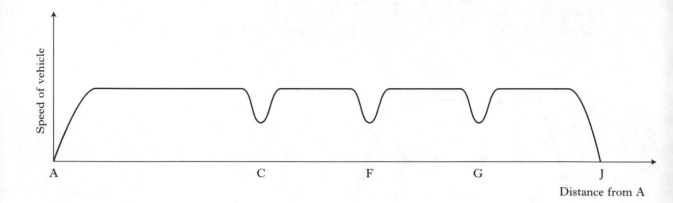

8. (a) -42 (b) (i) $2x(x-3)$ (ii) $\dfrac{2x}{x+3}$

9. (a) $\dfrac{7^2 \times 8^2}{4}$ (b) $\dfrac{n^2 \times (n+1)^2}{4}$ (c) $\dfrac{n^2 \times (n+1)^2 - 7^2 \times 8^2}{4}$

10. (a) $L = kD\sqrt{S}$ (b) 42 litres

11. (a) $6a^2 - 17ab + 5b^2$ (b) $x = -\dfrac{1}{2}$ or 5 (c) $x = 26$

12. $GE \doteqdot 64$ km

13. $a = 2$; $k = 3$

14. (a) 20 (b) Proof (c) $2q - p = 5$ (d) $p = 1$; $q = 3$

15. (a) $10\sqrt{2}$ (b) $2y^3$

16. (a) $2 \cdot 2$ m (b) $1 \cdot 75$ m (c) After 2 seconds

1. £101

2. (a) X   (b) X, because graph shows two rates of descent

3. (a) 0·75 m   (b) 7·2 m^3

4. (a) 9 × 17   (b) $n(2n-1)$

5. $y = 2x + 1$

6. 5 cm

7. (a) 2·48 m   (b) 26·72 m

8. 4·7 m

9. (a) £68   (b) $C = 4p + 6(d-2)$

10. 409·7 m

11. (a) $a = 1·5; b = -2·5$ (b) $k = dt + m$ (c) $x = 0$ and $x = 7$

12. 16·6 m

13. (a) $T \alpha \dfrac{S}{E}$ or $T = k\dfrac{S}{E}$ (b) 18 minutes

14. (a) $(15 \times 3) - (1 \times 17) = 28$ {other answers possible}
    (b) Prove that $(n+14)(n+2) - n(n+16) = 28$ where n is top left hand number in square

15. $x = 73·4$ and $286·6$

16. $v = 13$

17. (a) $(2a + 3b)(2a - 3b)$ (b) $\dfrac{1}{6}x$

18. (a) 19·2 m   (b) 19 m

19. (a) $2\sqrt{3} - 2$ (b) b

FREQUENCY CHART FOR CREDIT PAPERS

TOPICS	1993 Paper	1994 Paper	1995 Paper	1996 Paper	1997 Paper	1998 Paper
NUMBER						
Calculations	2	2	8	14		
Approximation						
Index Notation			2			
Ratio						
Distance Speed, Time	18	7				
Money	10			5,12	5	1
Time	113					
SHAPE						
Similarity	9		4			6
Co-ordinates						5
Area & Volume		14		2,9	2	3
Pythagoras	12	5	14		6	8
Angle Properties		4				
Shape Properties	1	10,20	6	3	1	7
Trigonometry	11,14,16	3,13,17	9,12,17	9,11,13,15	4,12,13,16	10,12,15,18
RELATIONSHIPS						
Patterns	6	6,15	10,19	17	9	4,14
Brackets	15(a)	9(a)		18(b)	11(a)	
Factorisation	8	9(b)	11(c)	10(a)	8(b)	17
Indices & Surds	17	18	11(b)	16(a)(b)	15	19
Formulae	4(b),13	16	3,16	4,16(c)	3	9(b),11(b)
Variation		12	18	6	10	13
Graphs & Tables	4(a), 5	8	5,7	7,8	7	2,9(a)
Equations	7,15(b)	1,19	1,13,15	10(b)(c), 18,19	11(b)(c),14	11(a)(c),16
Inequations				1		
Functions	17(a)		11		8(a)	
Linear Programming		11				

Printed by Bell & Bain Ltd., Glasgow, Scotland.